NORTHWICH, WINSFORD & MIDDLEWICH

THROUGH TIME

Paul Hurley

AMBERLEY PUBLISHING

Author Information

Paul Hurley is a freelance writer, author and is a member of the Society of Authors. He has a novel, newspaper and magazine credits, and a Facebook group titled Mid Cheshire Through Time, upon which all are welcome. Paul lives in Winsford, Cheshire, with his wife Rose. He has two sons and two daughters.

Contact: www.paul-hurley.co.uk

Email: hurleyp1@sky.com

Books by the same author

Fiction

Waffen SS Britain

Non-Fiction

Middlewich (with Brian Curzon)
Northwich Through Time
Winsford Through Time
Villages of Mid Cheshire Through Time
Frodsham and Helsby Through Time
Nantwich Through Time
Chester Through Time (with Len Morgan)
Middlewich & Holmes Chapel Through Time
Sandbach, Wheelock & District Through Time
Knutsford Through Time
Macclesfield Through Time
Cheshire Through Time

First published 2014

Amberley Publishing
The Hill, Stroud, Gloucestershire, GL5 4EP
www.amberley-books.com

ISBN 978 1 4456 3670 2 (print)
ISBN 978 1 4456 3688 7 (ebook)

British Library Cataloguing in Publication Data.
A catalogue record for this book is available from the British Library.

Typesetting by Amberley Publishing.
Printed in Great Britain.

Introduction

Mid Cheshire is a beautiful part of the country and this is the twelfth book that I have had the privilege of compiling. Despite this, none of the photographs in this book have been used in my previous publications. This is the latest of my *Through Time* books, and can be enjoyed in conjunction with those already in the shops. The book takes the reader on a journey into and through the town of Northwich, the epicentre of spectacular subsidence a hundred or so years ago as a result of wild brine pumping. Buildings collapsed or simply slid into the ground, so a unique answer was found for all new-build houses and shops in the town. They were built in such a way that they could be jacked back up and underpinned, should they begin to slip a few feet. These buildings were mainly wood framed with bricks inset, and the majority were painted in black and white, giving the town a rather unique and faux-ancient look. One genuine black-and-white building is Winnington Hall, built in the late sixteenth or early seventeenth century and added to some years later with a sandstone extension. This beautiful country house later found itself not in the country, but in the centre of an industrial complex. It was bought by John Brunner and Ludwig Mond, who wanted the estate to build their chemical works, Brunner Mond Ltd, later ICI. Initial plans to demolish Winnington Hall were later rescinded, and Brunner and Mond moved into it with their families. It later became a girls' school, then a social club for the workers, and is now a series of offices for small businesses. The hall has outlived most of the chemical works that once surrounded it.

All of the locations on our travels are snapshots in time. These introductions are not in chronological order, but give an insight into what can be found within the pages. From the town of Northwich, we meander through the surrounding villages of Mid Cheshire, such as the chocolate-box-pretty Great Budworth, with its ancient church and stocks. Time seems to have stood still in the village, with many genuinely old black-and-white cottages. The Winnington Turn Bridge is the site of the last actual battle in the English Civil War, known as the Battle of Winnington Bridge, when Sir George Booth's attempted rebellion was well and truly beaten by the Parliamentarians under Major General John Lambert. During these journeys, we come to the village of Hartford, and the Birtwisle car dealership that was well known for many years, but now no longer exists. Onwards through Whitegate, once home to the biggest Cistercian monastery in Europe, we now find a golf club. We also enter Winsford, a town that was once an industrial hotchpotch of Dickensian smog, poverty and hard graft, with its shipbuilding, salt mines and mills, one of which burnt down with sad loss of life. Little Budworth, another pretty village close to Winsford and home of the Oulton Park racing circuit, is captured in some quite unique old photographs. Delamere, in what was the ancient forest of Mara and Mondrem, is now a pleasant destination for hikers and those who enjoy the countryside.

On our Mid Cheshire trip, we take a look at the good old days of British Railways, including the long-lost station of Minshull Vernon. Our final destination is Middlewich, which we will approach via The Smoker public house. The Smoker was once located in a quiet backwater, albeit an important and ancient turnpike that now forms the A556 dual carriageway. Between 1939 and 1957, fighters took off from the airfields at Byley in order to protect the cities of Manchester and Liverpool. Although two previously published photographic books on Middlewich have made unused historical photographs hard to come by, the town deserves a mention nonetheless. It is famed as the site of the First and Second Battles of Middlewich during the English Civil War. Nine months after Sir William Brereton's Parliamentary forces had trounced the Royalists under Sir Thomas Aston, the town and church endured another battle. This time, Sir William was not so lucky. Facing a Royalist army of far superior strength boosted by troops from Ireland, he was beaten. So ended the Second Battle of Middlewich.

Acknowledgements

To compile a book such as this when I have already completed twelve similar volumes meant acquiring at least another ninety-two old photographs, and I would not have been able to do this without the valued help of the following people: Richard Rawlinson, John Evans, Trish Johnson, Geoff Dodd, John and Lesley Parker, Craig Singleton and his excellent website (http://www.rafcranage.org.uk), Alex Birtwisle, Denise Kendrick McNeel, Francesca Walton and Ben Brooksbank. To you all and anyone I may have missed out, many thanks for your help. Without you there would be no book.

I would like to thank my lovely wife, Rose, for her patience during the not inconsiderable time it took to complete the book and for her time spent with me taking the modern photographs and proofreading the end product. All modern photographs were taken by the author. The old ones were taken by an assortment of photographers to whom we are forever indebted, for without them we would not have these windows into the past.

Burrows Hill, 1911 and 2014

Let us start this tour through Mid Cheshire with a photograph of Burrows Hill and the ancestors of Trish Johnston, who kindly provided the photograph. The view looks up Burrows Hill towards Beach Road. The photograph was taken around 1910, and the couple are Trish's grandparents, Sarah Alice (Boden) Rathbone and Henry Clifford Rathbone. The infant is her father John Hayden, who was born in April 1910. What a lovely snapshot in time, taken in an area that is not usually visited by photographers, especially in the early 1900s.

Birtwisle's Car Showroom, 1938 and 2014

Birtwisle car dealership, based at Hartford, was a very well known Cheshire business that started as a blacksmith's in Hartford village. There will be a photograph of this later in the book, but here we can see two of the showrooms. In this pairing, we see the showroom that was situated opposite Hartford College. The photograph above was taken in 1938, and takes us back to the cars of the day. This busy photograph is filled with petrol pumps, contemporary attire and advertisements. The showroom went on to be a petrol station and, at the time of writing, is derelict.

Birtwisle's Car Showroom, 1973 and 2014
In this pair of photographs, Birtwisle car dealership is shown in the other premises further up Chester Road. One photograph depicts modern cars, still classics today, which were for sale in the 1970s. The business was sold by the Birtwisle family to Barber's car dealership in 1987, and the premises still trades as a garage, despite no longer remaining under the proprietorship of the Birtwisle family.

Castle Congregational Church, Undated and 2014

Continuing along Chester Road into Northwich, we find at the top of Castle Hill the fine red-brick Congregational church building. Founded in 1708 in Cross Street, Northwich, the church was rebuilt in 1852 as a 'neat and handsome chapel' on the plot now occupied at the bottom of Castle Street by Mosshaselhurst Solicitors. The 1852 church suffered greatly from subsidence and had to be demolished before being replaced in 1882 by the one in the photograph. This closed as a church in 2004 and has been redeveloped as dwellings.

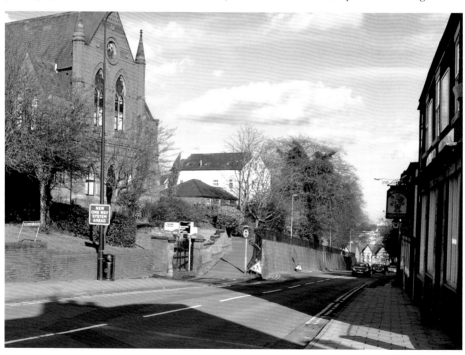

Lower Castle Street, Late 1800s and 2014
Having descended Castle Hill, we look back and see the Wheatsheaf public house (on the left in the old photograph). In the modern photograph, at the top of the hill, we find the spire of Holy Trinity church, built by the Weaver Navigation church in 1842. In the old photograph, we see the result of subsidence, one of many examples in an area devastated by this recurring problem.

Castle Street, Northwich.

Lower Castle Street, Early 1900s and 2014

Here we turn around and look towards Northwich to an area called Holloway. At the time of the old photograph, the Congregational church had been replaced by the current building. All of the buildings on the left, other than the aforementioned church, would shortly succumb to subsidence and be replaced. The building next to Mosshaselhurst, which was later to become a garage and petrol station, still stands today after having been a car showroom, carpet shop, nightclub and now a locksmith's.

Winnington Lane, Early 1900s and 2014

Crossing town, we now find ourselves in Winnington Lane with the intention of entering the town via Castle Street, better known as Castle Hill. The old photograph, hand coloured like the last one, shows the junction of Winnington Lane and Solvay Road. The residents at this time would primarily have been employed at the Brunner Mond chemical works. The church, St Luke's, would have been quite new at the time of the photograph. It was built to replace a 'tin church' in 1897 and had its gateway in Dyar Terrace.

Northwich Infirmary, c. 1900 and 2014

Now the Victoria Infirmary, the original mansion house, as seen in the photographs, was the home of salt magnate and local MP Robert Verdin, who donated it in 1887 for use as a local hospital. The grounds were also donated to the local council and became Verdin Park. They include a statue of Sir Robert Verdin. The hospital has been vastly expanded and still serves the people of Northwich today.

Lower Winnington Street, 1960s and 2014

Leaving the hospital, we continue down Winnington Hill and find, at the bottom, the location of one of the most famous old shops in Northwich. The second-hand shop, built in the 1600s as two cottages, was owned by Joe Allman. Joe was a local character and had the old shop stacked floor to ceiling with what some would call antiques and others might call junk. It had a soil floor and was deemed by the council to be unfit for human habitation. Instead of preserving this (once-thatched) local treasure, they pulled it down, along with the barrel-roofed building next to it. Joe was there for forty-odd years until the age of ninety.

New Bridge, Northwich

28992.

Northwich Town Bridge, *c.* 1900 and 2014
Looking across at the newly opened Town Bridge at the bottom of Winnington Hill, we get a better view of the church of the Holy Trinity, built by the trustees of the Weaver Navigation for use by the watermen who ply the river. These churches, like the one in Winsford, were ordered by an Act of Parliament to ensure that the boat families attended church. The vicar from 1926, later vicar of Northwich parish church, St Helens, was Alfred William Maitland-Wood MA. He was a well-known local worthy, who wrote two books on St Helen's church in 1937 and 1956.

Northwich Town Bridge, 1950s and 2014

We can now see the same bridge from the Winnington Street side. The bridge, built in 1899, is worthy of note because it was the second of its type, the first being Hayhurst Bridge in Chester Way, which was built in 1898. Both bridges, designed by Col. John Saner, were the first two electrically powered swing bridges in Great Britain and were built on floating pontoons to counteract the subsidence. As can be seen in the modern photograph, the height restriction has been raised to allow for high-sided vehicles, and the traffic is now one way due to a complete reworking of the road system in Northwich. These changes, in progress at the time of writing, are not necessarily popular with local people.

Northwich Bullring, Early 1900s and 2014

Observing Town Bridge from the Bullring side, we can see that this ancient centre of Northwich town was a hub for traffic passing through. As can be seen in the 2014 photograph, there is evidence of these controversial road changes in the form of plastic barriers. In the older photograph, a policeman stands by the large lamp standard in his shako hat, the predecessor of the peaked cap and later the helmet.

Parrs Bank, 1891 and 2014

This building is in Dane Street, between the Bullring and the bridge over the River Dane that can be seen in the photograph. Having been devastated by subsidence, this area was rebuilt to prevent future damage. Although it has met with occasional cases of flooding, it has lasted to become the attractive building that we see today. Note the addition of one window over the years.

The Bridge Inn, 1891 and 2014

Now here is an interesting bit of Northwich history. The ancient Bridge Inn shown in the old photograph is already showing signs of subsidence, and this was to become far worse, ultimately requiring the complete demolition of this building and those alongside it. In the new photograph, we can see a different building, which, despite weighing 50 tons, was moved 185 feet on rollers to take the place of the old inn in 1913. To get an idea of the location, see the inset photograph of the old mill that stood alongside the Bridge Inn, the corner of which can be seen in the mill photograph.

Northwich High Street, 1950s and 2014

We look now from the Bullring into the High Street at the policeman on duty directing traffic. The building on his left, M. Wood & Co., has been demolished to make way for Weaver Way and then Barons Quay Road and Leicester Street. In the new photograph, the long-closed and semi-derelict bar called The Amber Lounge is being redeveloped. The tall-fronted building beside the van is the old Eagle & Child pub, now a bank.

The Regal, 1950s and 2014

This well-known Northwich Regal Cinema has now been demolished and the area redeveloped as a Waitrose supermarket. At the time when the old photograph was taken, a film was being shown of the Queen's Coronation. This once-busy side of London Road is now mainly car parks and was once the site of the UK's only floating hotel, The Flotel, a short-lived hotel built on the river that closed in 2009 when the owners went into administration.

The Market Hall, 1897 and 2014

This large and typical Northwich market hall was built in 1843 and served the town well for many years. Corn was sold from The Crown & Anchor in Crown Street, and cattle from the cattle market in Church Walk. When the town was redeveloped in the 1960s, the old market hall, together with many other longstanding and loved buildings, was swept away to the chagrin of many people. They felt, with good cause, that the hall's replacement fell far short of worthy comparison. The Memorial Hall and the Court, built in the 1960s, have also been demolished.

The Bleeding Wolf, 1891 and 2014

This public house (now demolished), the side of which can be seen in the old photograph, was situated next to the market hall. A once busy area, it was cleared away to build the new market hall and the 'precinct'. The pub was built in 1776 as a private residence and became a very busy public house the following year. Situated as it was at the junction of Crown Street and Market Street, it was in the centre of Northwich's shopping and trade district.

Crown Street, 1895 and 1902

As we leave Market Street and head for Witton Street, we pass through the short Crown Street and see some of the shops that were once there. John Williamson Joynson, who also had a shop in Witton Street, can be seen selling groceries at Nos 7/9 Crown Street. Note how he takes advantage of his close proximity to the town market by advertising as 'The New Market'. I have included above some 1902 advertisements in place of a 'now' photograph, as the exact location is difficult to pinpoint.

Northwich High Street, 1960s/1970s and 2014

Here, we look up the High Street towards the Crown Street junction, where the road becomes Witton Street. The old Lennon's supermarket has now become a nightclub, and the old pub opposite, The Beehive, has been closed and is shuttered at the time of writing. This area has suffered greatly from flooding over the years, and the Lennon's building has acquired another first-floor window with an extension to take in the Lloyds TSB bank.

Witton Street, 1892 and 2014

As we move into Witton Street, Northwich's main shopping street, we can see that some buildings remain, whereas others have been replaced by examples of modern architectural excellence. Here we see Bradley's Hosier and Clothier at No. 19 and Samuel Moreland, ironmonger, at No. 23. The Edinburgh Woollen Mill and two charity shops now take their place.

Witton Street, 1950s and 2014
Turning around, we glance up Witton Street while a carnival procession is taking place. New Day furnishings and Boots, respectively, stand at the junction, with Leicester Street, or what is now a continuation of the pedestrian walkway, leading to the ancient and once poverty-stricken Leicester Street.

Witton Street, 1960s and 2014

This busy thoroughfare was, at the time, open to traffic in both directions. On the left is Bratt's Department Store. Henry Bratt opened his first shop, H. Bratt & Son, in Northwich in 1860. He later formed a partnership with his fabric buyer, Jack Evans, and the business was renamed Bratt & Evans Ltd. It continued to trade and serve the people of Northwich and its environs over the years, and has now had a third name change to simply Bratt's department store, with branches in Nantwich, Birkenhead and Knutsford. A true Northwich institution.

Witton Street, 1950s and 2014

Continuing up Witton Street at the time of the Northwich Carnival, we see parading towards us the Birkdale dance troup known as the Birkdale Dancers. The library is a little further along on the left, and the large building on the right is The Penny Black pub, once the main post and sorting office.

Next to the Plaza, Undated and 2014
Further up Witton Street now, we reach the gaudily painted Plaza Bingo Hall, once the cinema. Next door to it is this small shop, shown in the old photograph, housing the newsagent's, sweet shop and tobacconist's of Miss Sarah J. Patten. The building that can be seen on the left has now gone, making way for Venables Road.

Witton Street, 1892 and 2014

Past the Plaza now and almost opposite St Wilfrid's old school and church, this excellent period photograph shows women in their Victorian dresses standing outside the shop. The roof looks different in the new photograph, indicating some rebuilding over the years, but the match is perfect. The window of the top right of the gable end is still there.

The Cock, 1892 and 2014

As we continue up Witton Street, we pass through an area that was badly affected by subsidence. On the right, we come to a very attractive, modern-looking pub with the words The Cock Hotel and a bantam cock in mosaic on the front. For many years, this was a busy pub in a busy area, but now it all seems a bit bleak. The ancient pub in the old shot succumbed to subsidence and was demolished. The new one was later built, but with the decline of pubs it became unprofitable, and shortly after the turn of the present century it closed. It is now boarded up, although there is a sign on the side indicating that it is a prescription point.

Entrance to Northwich Station.

Northwich Station, c. 1910 and 2014

Further along Station Road, we come to the station after which it was named, built by the Cheshire Lines Committee in 1897; the line had opened from Knutsford in 1863. Later, it was expanded locally with salt-branch lines spreading out to the many salt mines in the area. Now, a Tesco supermarket and car park cover the site of the marshalling yard, and Northwich engine shed has been replaced by a housing estate.

St Helens Church, Northwich, 1900 and 2014

A casual stroll brings us to the Northwich parish church of St Helens, erected around 1560. The roofs, which are richly carved, date from 1686 to 1688. It is also known as Witton church, from the days when it was situated in Witton cum Twambrooks. The church was originally a chapel of ease to St Mary & All Saints at Great Budworth, which we will look at a little later. Comparing the two photographs, we see just how many gravestones have since disappeared.

Witton Cemetery, Late 1800s and 2014

Looking around the churchyard with the benefit of a late nineteenth-century hand-tinted photograph, we see again the difference in the number of gravestones, this time with more in the new photograph. The reason for this is simple – in the old photograph they simply did not exist. The cross in the foreground was there but was soon surrounded by others. Many of these have now been pulled over in the name of health and safety.

Comberbach Old Post Office, c. 1900 and 2014

Here we see another picturesque Mid Cheshire village situated on the Warrington/Northwich road, and what was once the village post office. This sixteenth-century building once housed Comberbach post office, which has now been relocated. This pretty row of cottages now hides somewhat behind the hedge, unlike at the turn of the last century when it was dressed in ivy. Rather than being demolished like so many other ancient buildings, these buildings have been brought up to a standard expected today, while retaining their historical appeal.

Winnington Hall, *c.* 1900 and 2014

Now we travel to Winnington, once a village in its own right but now part of Northwich. Here we find the old Winnington Works of ICI/Brunner Mond Ltd, but what is left is owned by Tata Chemicals. Here is a beautiful black-and-white hall attached to a sandstone one. The wooden-framed building is older than the sandstone extension. The original timber-framed house was built in the late sixteenth or early seventeenth century for a member of the Warburton family of Warburton and Arley Hall. In 1775, Samuel Wyatt designed what became the larger stone extension to the house. In 1872, the estate and hall, together with the land that was to be used for their chemical factory, were bought by John Brunner and Ludwig Mond, who both lived in it until around the late 1890s. The hall had been a girls' school, and after the First World War, the buildings were converted into a social club for the employees. Now it has been converted again into offices for rent.

Northwich Police Station, 1980s and 2014

I have included this relatively recent old view because of the changes that have been made. The first police station, a lock-up in Cross Street, was a small brick building with three cells. This was replaced by a large black-and-white police station that went on to be demolished before Northwich courthouse was built on the site. The one in the photograph was constructed in the 1960s on the other side of the road with a ramp at one end. This has been modernised, as can be seen below.

Winnington Bridge, Early 1900s and 2014

This narrow road bridge is situated on the A533 road from Northwich to Barnton. It was built in 1908, replacing the short-lived predecessor that is shown in the old photograph from the late 1800s. In the early 1900s, the bridge was listed and had the full title of Winnington Turn Bridge. In August 1659, a far older bridge was the scene of an important battle during Sir George Booth's uprising. This uprising was a failure and support was lacking. The Battle of Winnington Bridge was a scuffle, with Booth's Royalists holding the high ground on the other side of the bridge. Maj.-Gen. John Lambert's cavalry crossed the bridge and there was a short skirmish. Booth's forces were no match for Lambert's veterans. They scattered with only one of Lambert's men and about thirty of Booth's insurgents killed. This battle ended the uprising, and Booth escaped dressed as a woman but was later arrested in Newport Pagnell while having a shave.

Winsford Delamere Street and School, *c.* 1950 and 2014

Leaving the Northwich area, we now arrive at Winsford and its ancient Delamere Street. Once the centre of the parish of Over, where the mayor was second in seniority to the mayor of Chester, it is now part of Winsford. There have been a lot of changes in this area: in the new photograph we can see where buildings on the right have gone, making way for a new private estate and access road called Pinewood Road. The schools were built in 1840 at a cost of £500 for use as the Over Market Hall; they were later bought by Lord Delamere in 1858 and converted into a school.

Over Cross, Early 1900s and 2014

The old photograph shows the seventeenth-century once-thatched cottage that was demolished in 1972, causing upset to local historians. There were two ancient crosses in Over, but they were removed in the early 1800s. The Saxon cross, between the cottage and the school, was built in 1840 and contained a lock-up. It has been the subject of urban myths as to its construction date, and stories of the Devil carrying off St Chad's church. Even the council, when naming the nearby road, called it Saxon Crossway. Although this road has been bypassed, the heavy traffic that it still carries can be seen in the new photograph.

Delamere Street Farm, 1898 and 2014

Originally called School Farm, this building faced the road and had a barn next door. The farmer would have farmed fields that are now part of the Grange Estate at the rear. It later became a butcher's premises and was eventually demolished and replaced by the modern building, which does in fact look quite similar. On the left of this new building was the rebuilt White Lion pub. It had existed in Delamere Street from 1810 until it was demolished in the early 1960s when the new one was built. This, in turn, is now a convenience store.

Old Cottages in Delamere Street, Undated and 2014

These old cottages were situated approximately where Pinewood Road is now, as can be seen from St John's church spire to the right. These cottages were built in the 1600s and, like identical houses today, they were all similar in construction and style. It is possible to see the old cottage that was once by the cross and, further down still towards Over Square, the cottage that is still there. The chimneys and dormers all bear a similarity. Instead of being modernised, which would have retained the look of this ancient street, these were unfortunately demolished.

Winsford Church, Mid-1900s and 2014

This unusual church was designed by the famous architect John Douglas of Sandiway, and was only his second church. It was built as a congregational chapel in 1865, in what is technically called Polychromatic brickwork. Douglas' biographer described it as 'experimental' and 'an astonishing sight', whereas Nicholas Pevsner, the noted architectural historian, simply described it as 'very ugly'. Nicknamed 'the Streaky Bacon church', it did not appeal to the locals at the time either. The years have been kind, however, and I am not alone in seeing it as a very attractive building. The ancient white cottage was demolished in the 1960s. The road in the old photograph was once Swanlow Lane, but is now just the entrance to the church car park, having been bypassed.

Corner High Street and Well Street, 1960s and 2014

Along the dual carriageway, which used to be the narrow High Street and its junction with Well Street, was Thomas Bowyer's baker's shop at No. 459 High Street. Up to the eighteenth century, the people of Over drew their water from a well at the end of what became Well Street (for obvious reasons). This road later joined up with Queensway and led through to Weaver Street and Way's Green.

Plumbley's Yard, Dingle Lane, 1920s and 2014
This was the longstanding stonemasonry business of Frederick Plumbley, situated at No. 150 Dingle Lane. The business existed in 1914 and only closed recently when the business changed hands.

Ways Green, *c.* 1900 and 2014

Now we pay a visit to Ways Green, the road that leaves the junction with Weaver Street and Dingle Lane and drifts into the countryside and down to the banks of Winsford Flashes. In the old image, not the best of photographs but worth using for its antiquity, it has been snowing. The houses here would have been quite new at that time, and building work is again being carried out in the area as a private estate is being built nearby. In the old photograph, the circular wall enclosed a large house called Fern Villa, now the Conservative Club. For a while, a building in the grounds was the Catholic church, prior to the new one on Woodford Lane being built.

Queensway, 1949 and 2010
Back now to what was then the recently built Dene Estate, one of the first and arguably the best of the post-war council estates. The crossroads are now controlled by a mini-roundabout and the hedges and trees have grown, taking away the bleakness of the new estate. Original plans for the area around Dene Drive crossroads to become a small shopping centre were abandoned prior to completion.

Kennerley's Shop, 1950s and 2014

Here we are at the main crossroads on the dual carriageway between the High Street, Grange Lane and Dene Drive. The shop on the right was another longstanding Winsford business that, in 1934, was described as Cornelius Kennerley bakers. With the road widening, the shop had to go. As can be seen in the new photograph, its place has been taken by the widened Grange Lane, leaving the pair of semi-detached Edwardian houses as the first buildings after the junction.

Schools High Street, 1960s and 2014

This pair of photographs ably shows the difference in the High Street before and after the imposition of the dual carriageway in the 1970s. The houses and petrol station on the right have gone to make way for the developments, and the Queens Arms pub on the corner has been moved into Dene Drive.

Technical Schools High Street, 1897 and 2009

The Verdin Trust was set up in 1889 by Sir Joseph Verdin to compensate people for subsidence caused by brine pumping. In 1891, the Brine Pumping Compensation Act was passed, thereby rendering the trust redundant. The money was used to build the Verdin County School, opened in 1895. The name was changed from Verdin County School to Verdin Grammar School in 1935. It remained as such until 2010, when the Verdin school and the Woodford Lodge school were amalgamated and became The Winsford E-ACT Academy in new purpose-built buildings in Grange Lane.

Winsford Shopping Centre, 1970s and 2014

We now enter the much altered 1960s shopping precinct with its later name of Winsford Cross shopping centre. This part is called Fountain Court; as can be seen in the old photograph, it once had a fountain, although it is empty here. During the later alterations, the fountain was removed and the war memorials relocated to the area.

Winsford Old Baths, 2009 and 2014

After the old Winsford baths and gym were closed, I took a photograph, which included the Winsford Lifestyle Centre that was built behind it to replace it. Since 2009, like Northwich, Winsford has seen a lot of change. The Civic Hall has gone, the new Winsford E-ACT Academy has been built and the roads have been altered.

White Swan High Street, 1964 and 2014

A quick look now at this High Street pub that was built in 1869 and served the people of Winsford for nearly 100 years. It succumbed to road widening in 1964 when the old photograph was taken. A new White Swan was built in the same year on Wharton Road, serving the new council estate at Wharton. Later changing its name to Swannies, it is closed and awaiting sale at the time of writing.

Waterman's Church, *c.* 1900, and Advertisements From 1902

I have matched this photograph with local period advertisements, as there is little to see now and what is there can be seen in the next pair of photographs. Having already looked at Waterman's church in Northwich, we now have the Winsford one, Christ Church. Built in 1844 by the River Weaver trustees, it had to be demolished due to subsidence, and was rebuilt in wood and plaster in 1881. As churchgoing became less of a popular pastime and churches became warehouses, Christ Church lay derelict for a while before being demolished in the 1970s.

High Street and Queen Street Winsford, 1930s and 2014

What a snapshot of history this old photograph is. Winsford High Street was a densely populated area lined with shops of all descriptions in the mid-twentieth century. One of them was the one shown here at No. 402 Hugh Street, the cycle repair shop owned by Harry Oakes, who is in the doorway smiling for the camera. As can be seen in the modern photograph, all of this has now gone, leaving wasteland. I have included a local advertisement as an inset to add some interest to what is now a rather bland site.

High Street, 1890 and 2014

Looking down towards Town Bridge, we get a view of the Queen Street junction and Harry Oakes' shop, before he arrived on the scene. On the left, you can see the end of Christ Church wall, the short Queen Street leading to the council offices, and Hamlet's salt works on what is now the car park off New Road. The old photograph here shows just how busy this area was.

Lower High Street, Early 1900s and Early 2014
We have now reached the bottom of the High Street now and can look back to see Weaver Street on the left and New Road on the right. Before the bypass was built in the 1970s, this was the A54 and the main route for all traffic through Winsford. In the old photograph, the corner shop on the right is the chemist's, whose proprietor is shown as F. Clarke. By 1914, Mr Clarke is still listed as being in residence.

No. 22 High Street, 30 March 1893 and 2014
In an earlier image, the faded board on the front of this corner shop says that the proprietor is Frank Clarke. The shop later became R. Burgess, chemist, druggist and grocer, listed at Nos 22–24 High Street. The road off to the right is New Road.

Winsford & Over Station, Undated and 2014

The actual location of the station is unreachable, and was situated further behind the Navigation/Vale Royal/Liquid Lounge club. The new photograph shows the end of what is now the Whitegate Way country park. The station was built shortly after the line was constructed in 1870, mainly to link the salt mines of Winsford to the Chester to Manchester line at Cuddington. The passenger service was never a massive success, and there was an intermediate station at Whitegate. The line closed to passengers in 1958 and to freight in 1966. The trackbed is now a very pleasant country walk.

New Bridge Salt Works, Early 1900s and 2014

At one time, salt workings lined both sides of the River Weaver at Winsford, and this one was at the far end below the village of Moulton. The whole area was one given to hard work, smoke, steam and muck, with mines and shipbuilding. Railway lines on one side of the river carried salt away via the Cheshire lines to Cuddington, and on the other side via the London & North Western Railway (LNWR) main line. Through the years, many salt flats and other coasters took the salt to Liverpool along the river and then across the world. The exact location of the old photograph was pointed out to me by a local gentleman who could recall the view as it once was.

Bottom of Weaver Street, 1970s and 2014

Here we are again among the tightly packed shops, clubs and houses at the bottom of Weaver Street and High Street. This area was swept away during the building of the dual carriageway in the 1970s. The first building on the left is the Conservative Club, which moved to Fern Villas in Ways Green. A little further on is the closed Magnet, one of Winsford's two cinemas. The Winsford Gasworks opened behind the buildings on the right in 1858 and the land upon which it stood now houses the Winsford Campus of Mid Cheshire College.

Winsford Bridge, 1910 and 2014

This photograph, taken around 1910, looks across the Town Bridge and up the High Street during a period when this part of the town was at its busiest. The blue metal bridge has not yet taken the place of the one in the photograph, but will soon do so. The new bridge was supported by bags of concrete that can still be seen from the river.

Wharton Road From the Bridge, 20 September 1892 and 2014

Here we get a view up Wharton Hill, or Wharton Road, to be exact. This ancient photograph oozes with antiquity and, accordingly, is not of a very good quality. The high blue-black brick wall on the right, which has now gone, has yet to be built. All the buildings, apart from those further down on the left, have gone. The path leading off on the right runs through to Hill Top Avenue.

Wharton Hill, *c.* 1960s and 2014
A later photograph shows Wharton Hill. Once known as Winsford Hill, its name was changed due to a hill of the same name in Winsford. In this old photograph, we look down towards Town Bridge before it became part of a massive roundabout. The high blue-black brick wall on the left supported the land above it. When the road was widened, this was removed and the landscaping behind it negated the need for the support.

Winsford Town Hall, 20 September 1892 and 2014

The town hall stands alongside the bridge and was built in 1872 using timber and plaster. Due to subsidence, it was raised by 8 feet in 1879 and the foundations were relaid. The market hall next door was built of brick in 1859 and partly rebuilt in 1879. The town hall building provided facilities for lectures, dancing and other social pursuits. When silent movies arrived, it was the first venue used to show them. Winsford boasted its own band called The Black Faced Minstrels. As time went on, while standing precariously above the crumbling riverbank, it became a dance hall called The Strand and a nightclub called Mr Smiths (a venue for everything from classical music to striptease). It was finally demolished in the 1970s.

Royal Oak Market Place, 1892 and 2014

This well known pub in the old market place became The Royal Oak in the 1780s and stood opposite the town hall in this busy and crowded area. It was opened in 1767 as The Cock, with James Staley as its first licensee. In the 1970s, it became The Bees Knees, with much plastic shrubbery and bees. Renamed Chasers in 1985, it reverted to De Bees, a play on Bees Knees, the name it currently holds.

Three Pubs, Market Place, 1892 and 2014

The Market Place, in days of old, was the nearest Winsford got to a red-light district. As well as the Royal Oak, there were seven pubs in this small area: the Ark, often called the Noah's Ark; the Red Lion; the three pubs seen in the old photograph (The Flatman's Cabin, the Ship and the Swan), and next to the Ark was a pub called the Coach and Horses. The latter pub was situated where the bookie's now stands. Opened in 1869, it was demolished in 1907 like many Winsford pubs.

Winsford Station, 1960s and 2009
This old photograph was taken in the 1960s when the West Coast main line was being electrified. Nearly all of the stations and bridges had to be altered to take the wires. This was the main and only remaining station in Winsford; Over & Winsford and Over & Wharton stations have now gone.

Over & Wharton Station, 1970s and 2009

This station was opened at the top of Wharton Hill on 3 July 1882. Like Winsford & Over, it was planned mainly to carry salt from the many works in the area on this side of the river. It did have passenger facilities, but only provided two trains a day to and from Hartford station on the main line. It closed to passengers in 1947 and to freight in 1991, after which the track was lifted and Wharton Park Road, the A5018, was built in its place. The Wharton Park pub and a small retail park were also built. The station buildings caught fire while they were disused during the 1970s, and the old photograph shows the fire being extinguished before the buildings were finally demolished.

Dalefords Lane, Marton, Mid-1900s and 2014

Time now to leave Winsford and look at some other locations, including Middlewich. We start here with Dalefords Lane, between Winsford and Sandiway. In the old photograph, taken in the mid-1900s, we see what a peaceful area this was. Now it is one of the main routes out of Winsford and is rather busy. In the distance is the seventeenth-century Beeches Cottage, and the black-and-white one on the right is also listed – pure, pretty Cheshire.

Whitegate Hill, 1920s and 2014

The view in the old photograph is from the road into Whitegate village towards the church. This road also leads to the ancient Vale Royal Abbey, as it was once called, where a golf club now stands. Over the course of time, the biggest Cistercian abbey has become a golf course. Buried in the churchyard is Sir Muirhead Bone, potentially the most famous war artist and etcher of the First World War, and his wife. During the Second World War, his serviceman son was at Vale Royal, a military hospital.

Delamere Post Office, 1950s/1960s and 2014

We now enter the picturesque village of Delamere and see the post office situated on the edges of Delamere Forest. The old photograph is dated by the Hillman Husky car coming out, and by the fact that the building was demolished about fifty years ago and rebuilt to form what we now see. The original old post office, in what was then one of the Crown Cottages and is now on the A556, is currently occupied by my in-laws. The business was relocated in 1927, as we see in the old photograph.

Little Budworth, *c.* 1900 and 2014

We now come across another pretty Cheshire village, Little Budworth. In the old photograph, we look towards the church on the left and The Red Lion pub on the right. There has been virtually no change over the period between the two images. The west tower of the church was erected between 1490 and 1526, at a time when church towers were built with stone and the remainder in wood. The body of the church was rebuilt in stone in 1800. In 1870/71, the interior was restored by John Douglas. Beer and Bible sat opposite each other in harmony.

Ancient and Modern, Little Budworth.

Little Budworth Old Post Office, *c.* **1920 and 2014**
This photograph is made all the more interesting by a little period humour. 'Ancient' refers to the children in the donkey cart, and 'modern' to the man on the 1910 vintage motorcycle and sidecar. The house was once Little Budworth post office, but is now a private dwelling. Apart from an extension and some sympathetic modernisation, not much has changed over the years.

Little Budworth Village Tree, 1920s and 2014

Entering the village from the opposite direction, we find the village tree, which, amazingly, still stands some ninety-odd years later. Apart from the building on the far left, not much has changed.

Little Budworth Vicarage Lane, Undated and 2014

Here we look back at the spot from which the last pair of photographs was taken and see that there has been some change here. I have marked the photograph as undated, but would estimate it as being sometime in the middle of the last century. The tree is on the far right with a cast-iron road sign. The buildings on the opposite side of the road have gone, and modern houses built in their place can be seen.

Egerton Arms, Little Budworth, 1960s and 2014

Another pub in the village, the Egerton Arms, began life in the 1700s as a one up, one down sandstone cottage belonging to the Earl of Shrewsbury. In 1797, it was first opened as an ale house with no changes until 1827 when, since accommodation was offered, it was recorded as The Board. By 1865, it was known as the Egerton Arms. In December 1917, it was sold to Sir Philip Grey-Egerton of Oulton Hall as a free and fully licensed inn. In the 1960s photograph, the hunt is setting off.

Oulton Park Entrance, Little Budworth

Oulton Park Gates, Mid-1900s and 2014

Viewing the lodge entrance to Oulton Park from the outside, this gateway was designed by Joseph Turner in the late 1700s. The Oulton estate was in the Egerton family from the Middle Ages, and the Tudor home that they lived in burnt down, so a new one was built in 1715 when the grounds were expanded and walled in. At 10 a.m. on 14 February 1926, the large stately home burnt down and six people died as a result of the fire. During the Second World War, US troops, including General Patton, were based on the land, and in 1950 the land was handed back to Sir Philip Grey Egerton. A few years later, it became an international motor racing circuit.

Inside Oulton Park Lodge Entrance, Mid-1900s and 2014

In this last look at Little Budworth, we see the lodge entrance from within. In the 2014 photograph, motorcycles roar around the quite prestigious Oulton Park motor racing circuit. In the old photograph, people are enjoying the quiet of the countryside and perhaps a little light refreshment inside the grounds of the Old Hall. I can assume that the hall might have burned down by this time. It was still a peaceful time for the park, a peace that was soon to be shattered when the Oulton Park Race circuit opened in the early 1950s.

Davenham War Memorial, 1921 and 2014

We now move onwards to Davenham, between Northwich and Winsford, where we have a photograph of the unveiling of the war memorial on 1 July 1921 by Captain W. H. France-Hayhurst of Bostock Hall. The school behind the memorial has now been relocated, and the building converted to dwellings.

Blue Cap, Sandiway, Northwich

The Blue Cap, Early 1900s and 2014

The ancient turnpike road from Chester to Manchester, situated on what is now the A556, once facilitated the mail coaches that travelled between the two cities and onwards. Hotels were used as staging posts for this traffic, an important example being the Sandiway Head Inn. This famous old inn, which stood on the foundations of an even earlier one, was later to have its name changed to The Blue Cap after a famous dog. The Sandiway Head Inn, built in 1716, welcomed local people and regular stagecoaches. On alighting from the coach, they would be met with the smell of wood smoke and the inviting glimmer of oil lights and candles from the small leaded-glass windows. Inside, the midwinter frost would give way to a blazing log fire and warm ale.

Hartford Village, *c.* 1900 and 2014

Into the village of Hartford, the sky in the modern photograph looks rather wild. It was taken during the spectacular storms of early 2014. In the old photograph, we can see the tip of the church spire through the trees. The cottages on the right are the only buildings in the foreground of both photographs. The previously featured Birtwisle car dealership started here as a smithy on the far left.

Hartford Station, 1960s and 2014

We now come to the first of a selection of railway photographs, the first two from the lens of photographer Ben Brooksbank. Continuing through Hartford, we come to Hartford station and look down from the road bridge to a workman on top of one of the waiting rooms that was built in the early 1960s as part of the West Coast electrification. In the station is Patriot class locomotive No. 45543 *Home Guard,* with a train heading for the north.

Through Hartford Station, 1960s and 2014

A train with a fitted freight has passed through Hartford, pulled by a Jubilee class engine No. 45613 *Kenya*. Due to inaccessibility and prickly bushes, the modern shot leaves a little to be desired.

Greenbank Station, 1890s and 2014

Continuing towards Northwich, we find another station on a different line. Initially called Hartford & Greenbank, its name was changed after about ninety years to Greenbank, due to the occasional mix-up with nearby Hartford station. As can be seen, the station has changed little over the years as people in Victorian dress join their train to Manchester. The station buildings, once the home of the stationmaster (who at the time of the old photograph was John James Griffiths), have now been converted into a church.

Minshull Vernon Station, 1958 and 2014

Once situated between Winsford and Crewe, this station has long since been closed and, apart from a few bricks, completely removed from the scene. In 1896, George Tanner was the stationmaster on this small main line station. In the 1958 shot, the station has long been closed, but the platform still remains as railway photographers catch two unique locomotives passing through with the *Royal Scot* for the south. These two engines were from the experimental D1000 and D1001 series. Built in 1947/48, they remained in service until 1963–66 and were scrapped in 1968.

Cuddington Station, 1920s and 2014

We now take a last look at our railway system with a 1920s photograph of another Cheshire Lines railway, Cuddington. Just a short distance further on is the branch to Winsford. The view is towards Manchester and, like most small stations on this line, the buildings have been put to another use (in this case, as a private dwelling). At the time of the old photograph, these small stations had a full staff, including a smart stationmaster. The stationmaster here in 1896 was George Stocks.

The Gate, Weaverham

Hanging Gate at Weaverham, Nineteenth Century and 2014

'This gate hangs well and hinders none refresh and pay and travel on.' These are the words that travellers over the years have looked up at as they read the inscription on the farm gate. The gate hangs from the wall of the old but beautifully presented pub, The Hanging Gate at Weaverham, on what was the main road from Whitchurch to Warrington. The actual age of this ancient building has been lost in the mists of time. Prior to 1827, it was called The Weaverham Gate, The Barrymore Arms and then, simply, The Gate. It has now reverted to The Hanging Gate and is an excellent modern pub with good food and drink.

Great Budworth, Early 1900s and 2014
We now enter Great Budworth, a quintessential English village and one of the most famous and pretty in Cheshire. With its narrow lanes and ancient cottages, it is a place where time seems to stand still. Sandstone and cobbles remain as a link with the past and all that was attractive about the English village. The old stocks can be seen in both photographs, and the church of St Mary and All Saints and the Lady chapel date from the fourteenth century.

Arley Hall Gate, Undated and 2014

The village of Arley is around 5 miles from Northwich, and Arley Hall is now open to the public, although it is still the home of Lord and Lady Ashbrook. The gardens are among the finest in Britain, and the farm on the estate is also open to the public, especially children who can pet and feed the animals.
The hall was built for Rowland Egerton-Warburton between 1832 and 1845. He was Viscount Ashbrook's great-great-grandfather and the house was built to replace an earlier one on the site. The photographs were taken from an avenue lined with lime trees. This is the main entrance and the clock, dating from the nineteenth century, has only one hand.

The Smoker, Early 1900s and 2014

In the village of Plumley, on what is now the busy A556 dual carriageway between Chester and Manchester, we find the ancient pub, The Smoker. It is believed to have been built during the time of Queen Elizabeth I. It became a coaching inn during 1611, and was named The Bell, The Shoulder of Mutton and The Griffin. Almost all of the inns along this stretch of what was once leafy Cheshire are named after racehorses, and this one is named after Lord De Tabley's white charger, the Smoker.

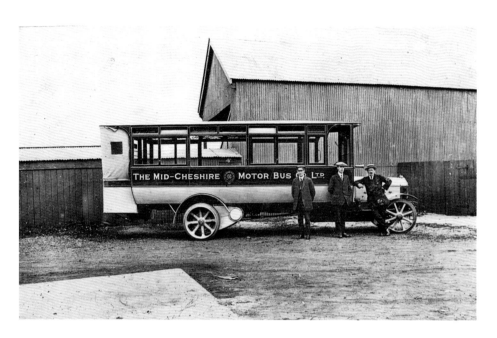

North Western Bus, c. 1915–20 and 1950s

I decided not to take an identical photograph of the North Western bus at the Three Greyhounds crossroads in Byley, as nothing has changed in the area. Instead, I have put old against new, from the period after the First World War to the 1950s. The North Western Road Car Company was formed in 1923 from other bus companies such as the Mid Cheshire Motor Bus Company, which it took over in 1924. The new company was given a base in Mid Cheshire, and the company was renamed National Travel (North West) in 1974, most of the routes having been taken over by Crossville. The pub on this crossroads, The Three Greyhounds, was the local pub during the Second World War for the hundreds of RAF personnel who passed through RAF Cranage nearby.

Byley Stores, 1956 and 2014

Still in the village of Byley and on the way to Middlewich, we pass through the village stores that were once in business there. They went on to be Byley Garage, now a private house. The area was very busy during the Second World War due to the proximity of RAF Cranage, an important airfield for fighter planes protecting the nearby cities of Manchester and Liverpool. There was also a flight training school there, and Wellington bombers were assembled at the base. There is an excellent website looking at the history of the airfield, which was built in 1939 and closed in 1957.

Middlewich, 1960s and 2014

We now make our way to the town of Middlewich and see it during one of its many facelifts (in this case during the building of St Michaels Way, the A54, which became the new road through town). The Wych, or Wich, at the end of Middlewich identifies it as a salt town. The town has an interesting history, from the Romans, who were garrisoned here, to the important First and Second Battles of Middlewich during the English Civil War.

Middlewich, 1960s/1970s and 2014

We now look towards Middlewich church and an area that was heavily fought over during the Civil War in two separate battles. The Royalists and Parliamentarians met in this area, when the Royalists were outnumbered and took refuge in the church, where many were slaughtered. This first battle on 16 March 1643 was won by Sir William Brereton and his Parliamentarians. The second battle took place nine months later when the Royalists, under Lord Byron, killed around 200 troops and saw off Sir William and his Parliamentarians. All of this occurred around and within the walls of the church of St Michael & All Angels.

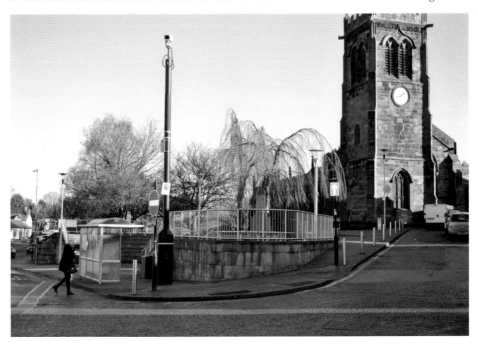

Wheelock Street, 1950s/1960s and 2014

In our final look at Middlewich, we see the main street, Wheelock Street, named after the river that flows through the town. One of the pubs in this area was the Red Cow, and it was in this hostelry that the bear known as Bruin would be taken to enjoy a drink. At the end of this street was the Bullring, a favourite place for bear baiting. A poem from the time reads,

> Scarce any man ever went sober to bed,
> 'Tis quite dreadful to think the lives they all led,
> At that time in Cheshire no fun could compare
> With the sport of all sports, namely, baiting the bear.

Enjoy the book and go through it again, there is always something you missed the first time.

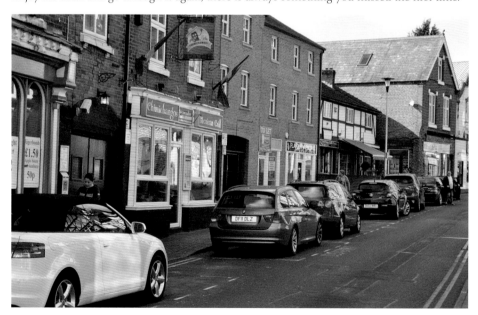